VOL. 6

HAL•LEONARD® KEYBOARD PLAY-ALONG

AUDIO ACCESS INCLUDED

ROCK Ballads

PLAYBACK+
Speed • Pitch • Balance • Loop

To access audio, visit:
www.halleonard.com/mylibrary

3917-6364-0583-1567

ISBN 978-1-4234-1796-5

Visit Hal Leonard Online at
www.halleonard.com

World headquarters, contact:
Hal Leonard
7777 West Bluemound Road
Milwaukee, WI 53213
Email: info@halleonard.com

In Europe, contact:
Hal Leonard Europe Limited
Dettingen Way
Bury St. Edmunds, Suffolk, IP33 3YB
Email: info@halleonardeurope.com

In Australia, contact:
Hal Leonard Australia Pty. Ltd.
4 Lentara Court
Cheltenham, Victoria, 3192 Australia
Email: info@halleonard.com.au

T0039906

HAL•LEONARD®

Visit Hal Leonard Online at **www.halleonard.com**

Explore the entire family of Hal Leonard products and resources

CONTENTS

Page   Title

4   Bridge Over Troubled Water
            SIMON & GARFUNKEL

10   Easy
            COMMODORES

17   Hey Jude
            THE BEATLES

21   Imagine
            JOHN LENNON

24   Maybe I'm Amazed
            PAUL MCCARTNEY

29   A Whiter Shade of Pale
            PROCOL HARUM

35   You Are So Beautiful
            JOE COCKER

40   Your Song
            ELTON JOHN

Bridge Over Troubled Water

Words and Music by
Paul Simon

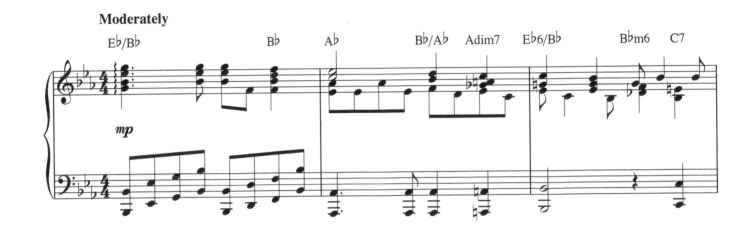

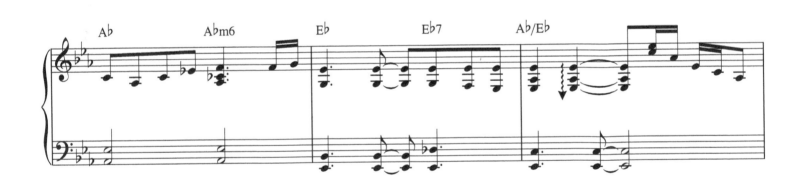

1. When you're wea - ry, _____
2. down and out, _____
3. *(See additional lyrics)*

When you're _

I will lay me down. _____

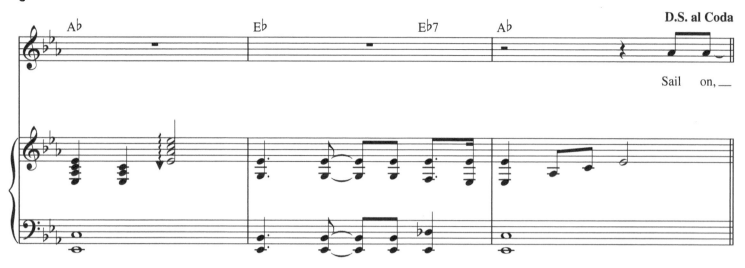

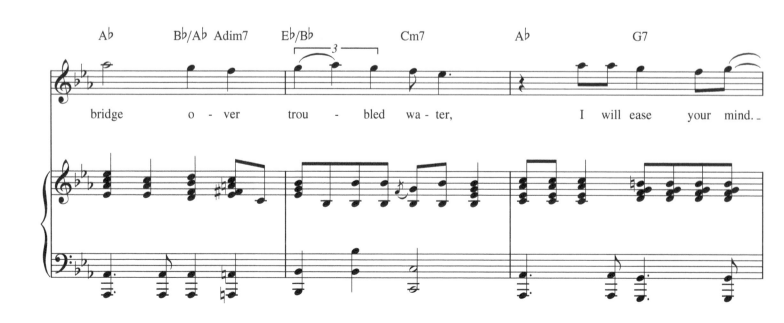

Additional Lyrics

3. Sail on, silver girl, sail on by.
   Your time has come to shine,
   All your dreams are on their way.
   See how they shine.
   Oh, if you need a friend,
   I'm sailing right behind.
   Chorus

Easy

Words and Music by
Lionel Richie

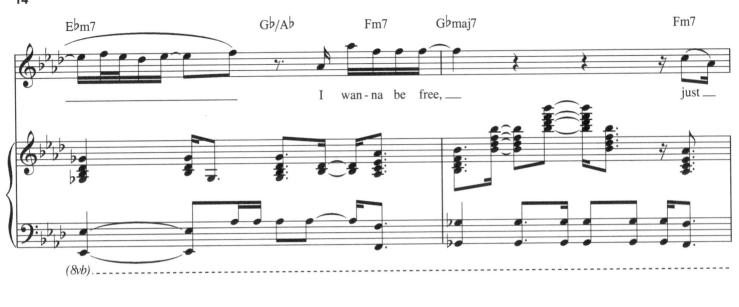

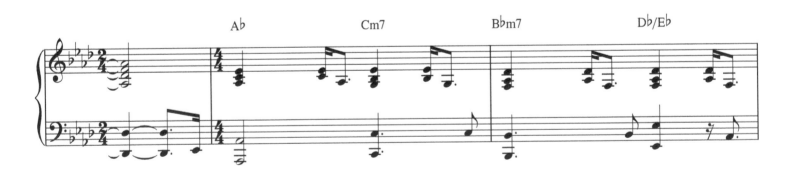

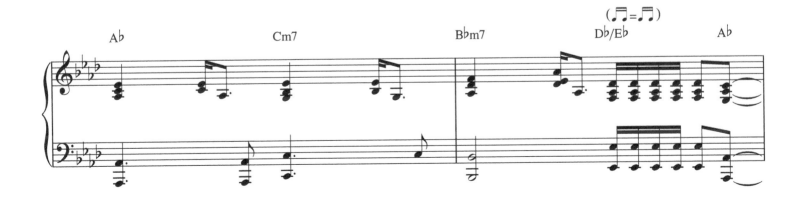

- y, _____ eas-y like Sun-day morn - ing.

'Cause I'm eas - y,

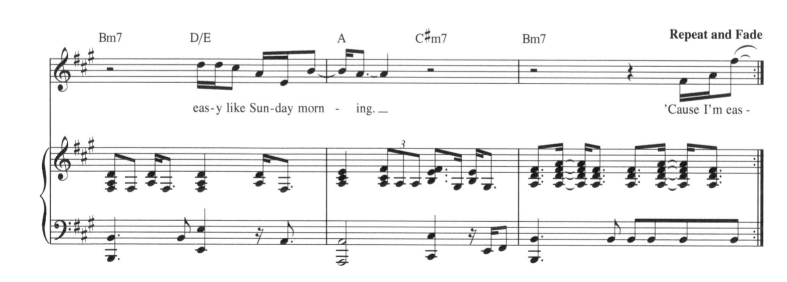

eas-y like Sun-day morn - ing. _____

Repeat and Fade

'Cause I'm eas -

Hey Jude

Words and Music by John Lennon
and Paul McCartney

Play 3 times

Na na na na na na na. Na na na na, hey, Jude.

Play 4 times

Na na na na na na na. Na na na na, hey, Jude.

Repeat and Fade

Na na na na na na na. Na na na na, hey, Jude.

Imagine

Words and Music by
John Lennon

No hell _____ be - low us, _____
Noth-ing to kill _____ or die _____ for,
No need for greed _ or hun - ger;

a - bove us on - ly sky.
and no re - li - gion too._____
a broth - er - hood of man._____

I - mag-ine all _____ the peo - ple _____
I - mag-ine all _____ the peo - ple _____
I - mag-ine all _____ the peo - ple _____

liv - ing for to - day. _____ Ah. _____
liv - ing life in peace._
shar - ing all the world._

Maybe I'm Amazed

Words and Music by
Paul McCartney

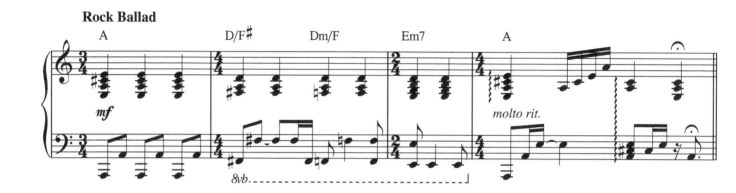

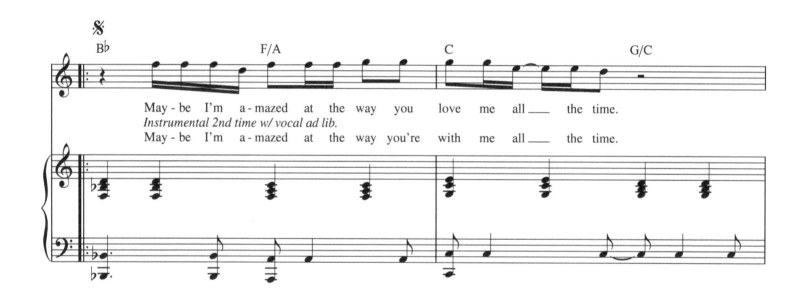

May-be I'm a-mazed at the way you love me all ___ the time.
Instrumental 2nd time w/ vocal ad lib.
May-be I'm a-mazed at the way you're with me all ___ the time.

May-be I'm a-fraid of the way I love ___ you.
May-be I'm a-fraid of the way I'd leave ___ you.

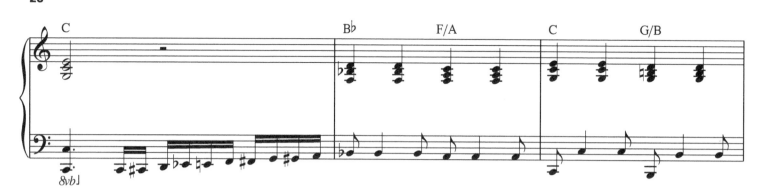

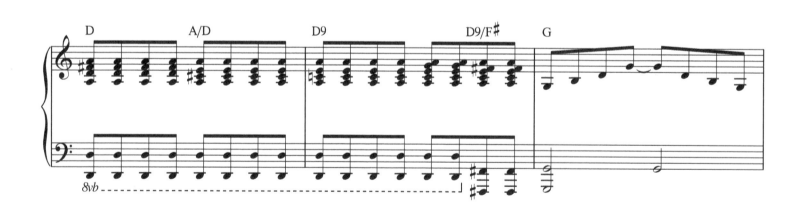

Fade out

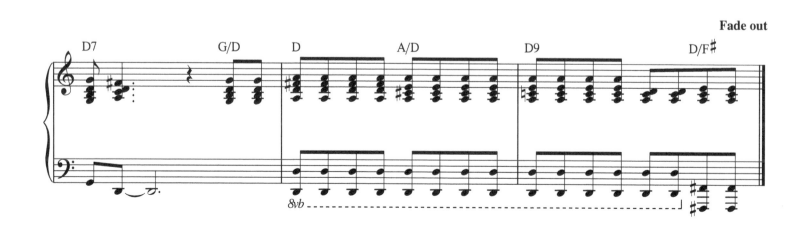

A Whiter Shade of Pale

Words and Music by Keith Reid
and Gary Brooker

*The Organ part has been arranged to be playable by one keyboard.
An Acoustic Piano comps throughout.

one of six - teen ___ ves - tal vir - gins who were leav-ing for the coast. _

And al-though my eyes _____ were o - pen,

they might just as well _ been closed. _ And so it was _____ lat -

- er, ___ as the mill - er told _ his tale, _

You Are So Beautiful

Words and Music by Billy Preston
and Bruce Fisher

Your Song

Words and Music by Elton John
and Bernie Taupin

I'd buy ___ a big house where ___ we both ___ could
it's for peo - ple like you that ___ keep it ___ turned ___

live. _____ If I was a sculp - tor, heh,
___ on. _____ So ex - cuse me for-get - ting,

but then a - gain, ___ no, or a man who makes po-tions in a
but these things I do. You see, I've for - got - ten ___ if they're green

HAL•LEONARD® KEYBOARD PLAY-ALONG

The **Keyboard Play-Along** series will help you quickly and easily play your favorite songs as played by your favorite artists. Just follow the music in the book, listen to the audio to hear how the keyboard should sound, and then play along using the separate backing tracks. The melody and lyrics are also included in the book in case you want to sing, or simply to help you follow along. The audio files are enhanced so you can adjust the recording to any tempo without changing pitch!

1. POP/ROCK HITS
Against All Odds (Take a Look at Me Now) • Deacon Blues • (Everything I Do) Do It for You • Hard to Say I'm Sorry • Kiss on My List • My Life • Walking in Memphis • What a Fool Believes.
00699875

2. SOFT ROCK
Don't Know Much • Glory of Love • I Write the Songs • It's Too Late • Just Once • Making Love Out of Nothing at All • We've Only Just Begun • You Are the Sunshine of My Life.
00699876

3. CLASSIC ROCK
Against the Wind • Come Sail Away • Don't Do Me like That • Jessica • Say You Love Me • Takin' Care of Business • Werewolves of London • You're My Best Friend.
00699877

6. ROCK BALLADS
Bridge over Troubled Water • Easy • Hey Jude • Imagine • Maybe I'm Amazed • A Whiter Shade of Pale • You Are So Beautiful • Your Song.
00699880

7. ROCK CLASSICS
Baba O'Riley • Bloody Well Right • Carry on Wayward Son • Changes • Cold As Ice • Evil Woman • Space Truckin' • That's All.
00699881

9. ELTON JOHN BALLADS
Blue Eyes • Candle in the Wind • Daniel • Don't Let the Sun Go Down on Me • Goodbye Yellow Brick Road • Rocket Man (I Think It's Gonna Be a Long Long Time) • and More!
00700752

10. STEELY DAN
Aja • Do It Again • FM • Hey Nineteen • Peg • Reeling in the Years • Rikki Don't Lose That Number.
00700201

13. BILLY JOEL – HITS
Allentown • Just the Way You Are • New York State of Mind • Pressure • Root Beer Rag • Scenes from an Italian Restaurant • She's Always a Woman • Tell Her About It.
00700303

16. 1970s Rock
Dream On • Highway Star • I Feel the Earth Move • Foreplay/Long Time (Long Time) • Point of Know Return • Sweet Home Alabama • Take the Long Way Home • Will It Go Round in Circles.
00700933

17. 1960s ROCK
Gimme Some Lovin' • Green Onions • I'm a Believer • Louie, Louie • Magic Carpet Ride • Oh, Pretty Woman • Runaway • The Twist.
00700935

Prices, contents, and availability subject to change without notice.

18. 1950s ROCK
Blueberry Hill • Good Golly Miss Molly • Great Balls of Fire • The Great Pretender • Rock and Roll Is Here to Stay • Shake, Rattle and Roll • Tutti Frutti • What'd I Say.
00700934

19. JAZZ CLASSICS
Blues Etude • (They Long to Be) Close to You • Freeway • Lonely Woman • My Foolish Heart • Tin Tin Deo • Watch What Happens.
00701244

22. CAROLE KING
I Feel the Earth Move • It's Too Late • Jazzman • (You Make Me Feel Like) a Natural Woman • So Far Away • Sweet Seasons • Will You Love Me Tomorrow (Will You Still Love Me Tomorrow) • You've Got a Friend.
00701756

24. DREAM THEATER
Breaking All Illusions • Erotomania • Fatal Tragedy • Hell's Kitchen • In the Presence of Enemies - Part 1 • On the Backs of Angels • Six Degrees of Inner Turbulence: I. Overture • Six Degrees of Inner Turbulence: II. About to Crash • Under a Glass Moon.
00111941

HAL•LEONARD®
www.halleonard.com

KEYBOARD *signature licks*®

These exceptional books and audio packs teach keyboardists the techniques and styles used by popular artists.
Each folio breaks down the trademark riffs and licks used by these great performers.

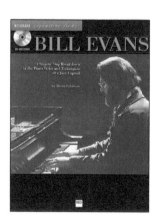
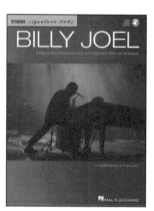

THE BEATLES

20 Beatles classics: All You Need is Love • Back in the U.S.S.R. • Don't Let Me Down • Good Day Sunshine • Hello, Goodbye • Hey Jude • In My Life • Let It Be • The Long and Winding Road • Ob-La-Di, Ob-La-Da • Penny Lane • Revolution • Strawberry Fields Forever • and more.
00329683 Book/Online Audio

BEST OF BLUES PIANO

by Todd Lowry

14 songs are covered: Big Chief (Professor Longhair) • Blueberry Hill (Fats Domino) • Cryin' in My Sleep (Jimmy Yancey) • Everyday I Have the Blues (Memphis Slim) • Honky Tonk Train Blues (Meade "Lux" Lewis) • The Pearls (Jelly Roll Morton) • Roll 'Em Pete (Pete Johnson) • Route 66 (Charles Brown) • Tipitina (Dr. John) • and more.
00695841 Book/Online Audio

BILL EVANS

by Brent Edstrom

12 songs from this jazz legend: Five • One for Helen • The Opener • Peace Piece • Peri's Scope • Quiet Now • Re: Person I Knew • Time Remembered • Turn Out the Stars • Very Early • Waltz for Debby • 34 Skidoo.
00695714 Book/CD Pack

BILLY JOEL

by Todd Lowry & Robbie Gennet

20 songs from the Piano Man: And So It Goes • Big Shot • The Entertainer • Honesty • Just the Way You Are • Lullabye (Goodnight, My Angel) • Movin' Out (Anthony's Song) • New York State of Mind • Piano Man • The River of Dreams • She's Always a Woman • She's Got a Way • Tell Her About It • Uptown Girl • more.
00345363 Book/Online Audio

OSCAR PETERSON PLAYS STANDARDS

by Brent Edstrom

A dozen classics: All of Me • Between the Devil and the Deep Blue Sea • Falling in Love with Love • Fly Me to the Moon • Georgia on My Mind • I Love You • In a Mellow Tone • It's All Right with Me • It's Only a Paper Moon • My Heart Stood Still • On the Sunny Side of the Street • When Lights Are Low.
00695900 Book/Online Audio

OSCAR PETERSON – CLASSIC TRIO PERFORMANCES

by Todd Lowry

14 of Oscar's trademark pieces: C-Jam Blues • Come Rain or Come Shine • Do Nothin' Till You Hear from Me • Don't Get Around Much Anymore • The Girl from Ipanema • I Got It Bad and That Ain't Good • The Lady Is a Tramp • My One and Only Love • Quiet Nights of Quiet Stars • Take the "A" Train • That Old Black Magic • and more.
00695871 Book/CD Pack

BEST OF ROCK

by Todd Lowry

12 songs are analyzed in this volume: Cold as Ice (Foreigner) • Don't Do Me Like That (Tom Petty & The Heartbreakers) • Don't Let the Sun Go Down on Me (Elton John) • I'd Do Anything for Love (Meat Loaf) • Killer Queen (Queen) • Light My Fire (The Doors) • Separate Ways (Journey) • Werewolves of London (Warren Zevon) • and more.
00695751 Book/CD Pack

BEST OF STEVIE WONDER

by Todd Lowry

14 of Stevie's best: Boogie on Reggae Woman • Don't You Worry 'Bout a Thing • I Just Called to Say I Love You • Living for the City • Master Blaster • My Cherie Amour • Overjoyed • Part Time Lover • Ribbon in the Sky • Send One Your Love • Sir Duke • Superstition • That Girl • You Are the Sunshine of My Life.
00695605 Book/CD Pack

Prices, contents and availability subject to change without notice.

HAL•LEONARD®

Visit Hal Leonard Online at
www.halleonard.com

THE NEW DECADE SERIES

Books with Online Audio • Arranged for Piano, Voice, and Guitar

The New Decade Series features collections of iconic songs from each decade with great backing tracks so you can play them and sound like a pro. You access the tracks online for streaming or download. **See complete song listings online at www.halleonard.com**

SONGS OF THE 1920s

Ain't Misbehavin' • Baby Face • California, Here I Come • Fascinating Rhythm • I Wanna Be Loved by You • It Had to Be You • Mack the Knife • Ol' Man River • Puttin' on the Ritz • Rhapsody in Blue • Someone to Watch over Me • Tea for Two • Who's Sorry Now • and more.
00137576 P/V/G

SONGS OF THE 1930s

As Time Goes By • Blue Moon • Cheek to Cheek • Embraceable You • A Fine Romance • Georgia on My Mind • I Only Have Eyes for You • The Lady Is a Tramp • On the Sunny Side of the Street • Over the Rainbow • Pennies from Heaven • Stormy Weather (Keeps Rainin' All the Time) • The Way You Look Tonight • and more.
00137579 P/V/G

SONGS OF THE 1940s

At Last • Boogie Woogie Bugle Boy • Don't Get Around Much Anymore • God Bless' the Child • How High the Moon • It Could Happen to You • La Vie En Rose (Take Me to Your Heart Again) • Route 66 • Sentimental Journey • The Trolley Song • You'd Be So Nice to Come Home To • Zip-A-Dee-Doo-Dah • and more.
00137582 P/V/G

SONGS OF THE 1950s

Ain't That a Shame • Be-Bop-A-Lula • Chantilly Lace • Earth Angel • Fever • Great Balls of Fire • Love Me Tender • Mona Lisa • Peggy Sue • Que Sera, Sera (Whatever Will Be, Will Be) • Rock Around the Clock • Sixteen Tons • A Teenager in Love • That'll Be the Day • Unchained Melody • Volare • You Send Me • Your Cheatin' Heart • and more.
00137595 P/V/G

SONGS OF THE 1960s

All You Need Is Love • Beyond the Sea • Born to Be Wild • California Girls • Dancing in the Street • Happy Together • King of the Road • Leaving on a Jet Plane • Louie, Louie • My Generation • Oh, Pretty Woman • Sunshine of Your Love • Under the Boardwalk • You Really Got Me • and more.
00137596 P/V/G

SONGS OF THE 1970s

ABC • Bridge over Troubled Water • Cat's in the Cradle • Dancing Queen • Free Bird • Goodbye Yellow Brick Road • Hotel California • I Will Survive • Joy to the World • Killing Me Softly with His Song • Layla • Let It Be • Piano Man • The Rainbow Connection • Stairway to Heaven • The Way We Were • Your Song • and more.
00137599 P/V/G

SONGS OF THE 1980s

Addicted to Love • Beat It • Careless Whisper • Come on Eileen • Don't Stop Believin' • Every Rose Has Its Thorn • Footloose • I Just Called to Say I Love You • Jessie's Girl • Livin' on a Prayer • Saving All My Love for You • Take on Me • Up Where We Belong • The Wind Beneath My Wings • and more.
00137600 P/V/G

SONGS OF THE 1990s

Angel • Black Velvet • Can You Feel the Love Tonight • (Everything I Do) I Do It for You • Friends in Low Places • Hero • I Will Always Love You • More Than Words • My Heart Will Go On (Love Theme from 'Titanic') • Smells like Teen Spirit • Under the Bridge • Vision of Love • Wonderwall • and more.
00137601 P/V/G

SONGS OF THE 2000s

Bad Day • Beautiful • Before He Cheats • Chasing Cars • Chasing Pavements • Drops of Jupiter (Tell Me) • Fireflies • Hey There Delilah • How to Save a Life • I Gotta Feeling • I'm Yours • Just Dance • Love Story • 100 Years • Rehab • Unwritten • You Raise Me Up • and more.
00137608 P/V/G

SONGS OF THE 2010s - Updated Edition

All About That Bass • Best Day of My Life • Cups (When I'm Gone) • Firework • Get Lucky • Happy • I Knew You Were Trouble • Just Give Me a Reason • Little Talks • The Middle • Perfect • Rolling in the Deep • Shallow • Stay with Me • There's Nothing Holdin' Me Back • Uptown Funk • Wake Me Up • and more.
00338996 P/V/G

halleonard.com

Prices, content, and availability subject to change without notice.